Chris Ronaldson, the world champion from 1981 to 1987.

Real Tennis

Kathryn McNicoll

A Shire book

To James

Published in 2005 by Shire Publications Ltd,
Cromwell House, Church Street, Princes Risborough,
Buckinghamshire HP27 9AA, UK.
(Website: www.shirebooks.co.uk)

British Library Cataloguing in Publication Data:
McNicoll, Kathryn
Real tennis. – (Shire album; 437)
1. Court tennis
I. Title
796.3'4
ISBN 0 7478 0610 1.

Cover: *Ballhouse of the Collegium Illustre, Tübingen. From the Stammbuch of Duke August the Younger of Brunswick, Luneburg (Herzog August Bibliothek, Wolfenbüttel. Cod. Guelf. 84.6 Aug.40.).*

ACKNOWLEDGEMENTS
The following people have been very helpful to me during the writing of this book and I would like to thank them all. They are, in alphabetical order, Roddy Bloomfield, Cees de Bondt, Tim Chisholm, Alistair Curley, Heiner Gillmeister, Karen Junod, Penny Lumley, Alistair McNicoll, James McNicoll, Valerie Morgan, Brian Rich, Bruce Ronaldson, Chris Ronaldson, Lesley Ronaldson, Mary Ronaldson, Adrian Snow, Peter Wordie and James Wyatt.
The following people have very kindly provided photographs for this book: Lord Aberdare (from his book *The J. T. Faber Book of Tennis and Rackets*), Martin Bronstein, Alistair Curley, Michael Do, Brian Dowling, Murray Glover, Tim Graham, Cadbury Lamb, Penny Lumley, Alistair and James McNicoll, Roger Morgan and Lesley Ronaldson.
Illustrations are acknowledged as follows: courtesy of Lord Aberdare, pages 25 (top), 29, 30 (both); Shelly Bancroft, page 31 (top); Bibliothèque du Musée Condé, Château de Chantilly, page 37; Bibliothèque Nationale de Paris, page 5; Martin Bronstein, page 34; Michael Do, page 36; Brian Dowling, pages 18 and 33 (bottom); Fundaçao Calouste Gulbenkian, Lisbon, page 4; *Le Globe Illustré*, page 25 (bottom); Murray Glover, pages 1, 3, 8, 11, 17 (both), 19 (both), 20; Tim Graham, page 35 (bottom); Herzog August Bibliothek, Wolfenbüttel, cover; Koninklijke Bibliotheek, The Hague, pages 9, 12; Cadbury Lamb, page 7; Penny Lumley, page 14; Alistair McNicoll, pages 23, 24 (bottom), 35 (top); James McNicoll, pages 21, 22 (both), 27; Roger Morgan, pages 15, 24 (top); Musée des Châteaux de Versailles et Trianon, page 29 (top); Lesley Ronaldson, pages 13, 31 (bottom), 32, 33 (top); Universitätsbibliothek Erlangen-Nürnberg, page 6.

Printed in Great Britain by CIT Printing Services, Press
Buildings, Merlins Bridge, Haverfordwest, Pembrokeshire
SA61 1XF.

Contents

Rob Fahey, the world champion from 1994.

The origins of real tennis

*The ball is much used by the nobility and gentry in their tennis courts and by the
people of meaner sort in the fields and streets.*

John Stow (1525–1605)

Most people, when they think of tennis, think of lawn tennis, the
game invented by Major Walter Wingfield in 1873, but a game called
tennis has existed for much longer. Nowadays this game is called
'real tennis' ('court tennis' in the United States of America) to
distinguish it from lawn tennis. Unlike lawn tennis, real tennis is
played in a specially constructed building or enclosed court.

The origins of tennis are obscure but the game is undoubtedly
very old. There is evidence to indicate that the Greeks were playing

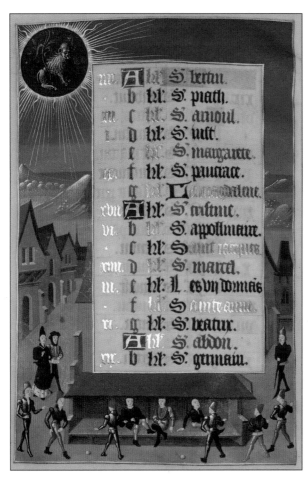

*Book of Hours, northern French,
1450–60. Note the two balls in the
court to show the two chases being
contended. (Fundaçao Calouste
Gulbenkian, Lisbon)*

A seventeenth-century engraving of a student with a tennis racket and balls. (Bibliothèque Nationale de Paris)

a very similar game as early as the sixth century BC and a game similar to tennis is described by the Greek grammarian Pollux in the second century AD. However, at a time when relatively few people could write, games were rarely considered important enough to be recorded in writing.

The oldest recorded tennis courts were those built for the gentlemen of the court in Valencia in Spain in 1298. Tennis is much better documented from the fifteenth century onwards in written references to the game and paintings. In 1415 the scoring in fifteens is described. The earliest account of the rules of tennis is given by Antonio Scaino in his *Trattato del Giuoco della Palla* ('Treatise on the Ball Game'), which was published in 1555.

For a long time it was believed that the game developed in monasteries and that the present-day court derived from the shape of the cloisters. Since the 1980s, however, when Roger Morgan investigated the game of *pallaeh!*, a game played in the village streets of Tuscany in Italy with rules remarkably similar to those of real tennis, there has been a reassessment of its ancestry. Many people now believe that tennis developed from a country game which probably moved from the countryside to the fast-developing towns in the thirteenth century, so as to secure a flat level surface on which to play. The shape of the modern court derives from the shape of the streets in which the game was played, and the penthouses (the

A seventeenth-century German tennis court; an engraving by Peter Aubry. (Universitäts-bibliothek Erlangen-Nürnberg)

roofed corridors surrounding the court) come from the sloping roofs and awnings of the shops. Moreover, monastic cloisters are square whereas tennis courts are considerably longer than they are wide.

However, most twelfth-century streets were very narrow and crooked, and only a few were wide enough and straight enough to accommodate a game of tennis. Many towns and cities also had strict rules about where games could be played, because the game was considered noisy and dangerous. Playing tennis also diverted the populace from more warlike sports such as archery, and many kings of France and England imposed bans on the game. It seems likely that these strictures were one of the reasons why tennis came to be played in an enclosed court. Other reasons were probably the filthy state of the streets in the Middle Ages and the desire of the nobility for a degree of privacy.

The move from open areas to an enclosed court was immensely influential to the game. None of the first courts, which were made of timber, has survived, but subsequent brick or masonry courts were often built on the same site. These early courts had no roofs, and pictures of them show a wide variety of arrangements for the penthouses and galleries. However, by the sixteenth century courts with penthouses and roofs were being built.

Most of the surviving information inevitably relates to courts belonging to royalty and the nobility, who had the time and money to build courts, but more modest courts, probably attached to inns, were available to ordinary people.

A further stage in the development of the game was the suspension of a cord across the middle of the court, first mentioned in the sixteenth century. It may have been introduced to separate players on opposing sides rather than control the flight of the ball. Later a net was added to distinguish good shots from bad.

The origins of the word 'tennis' are not known for certain but many people believe it comes from the French word *tenez*, which used to be the warning call given before putting the ball into play. This tradition of a warning call is still present in the Italian game of *pallaeh!* and also in the Basque game *rebot*.

The heyday of the game lasted from the end of the fifteenth century to the end of the seventeenth century. Most of the European royal houses had courts and there were courts in most major European towns. Paris alone had at least two hundred and fifty courts in this period.

There was a serious decline in the game in the eighteenth century, a revival in Victorian times, then a slump from the outbreak of the First World War until about the 1970s. Since then, however, there has been a marked renewal of interest in the game and old courts have been sought out and restored and new courts built. Although no new courts were built in England between 1912 and 1990 the building of a court at the Oratory School at Woodcote in Oxfordshire in 1990 has been followed by new courts at Chelsea Harbour (London), Bristol, Prested Hall near Kelvedon (Essex) and Hendon (London), with old courts being restored in Newmarket (Suffolk), near Bridport (Dorset) and in Cambridge. The game is thriving in Australia, Britain, France and the USA.

Built in 1885 and now restored, the court at Walditch, near Bridport, Dorset.

The Australian Rob Fahey, who became world champion in 1994.

The real tennis world championship is the oldest championship in the world and dates back to 1740. It takes the form of a challenge every two years. The top four contenders on the international ranking list are eligible to challenge the champion. They play a knockout series, and the winner of this makes the challenge. At the start of the twenty-first century an Australian, Rob Fahey, was only the twenty-fourth champion of the game.

Balls

...the barber's man hath been seen with him; and the old ornament of his cheek
hath already stuffed tennis-balls.
William Shakespeare, *Much Ado About Nothing*, Act 3, Scene 2

Early tennis balls were filled with organic material so there is little
archaeological evidence about them. It seems that, before the
introduction of rubber to Europe by Christopher Columbus at the
beginning of the sixteenth century, tennis balls were filled with such
materials as clay, plaster, chalk, sand and powdered egg shells and

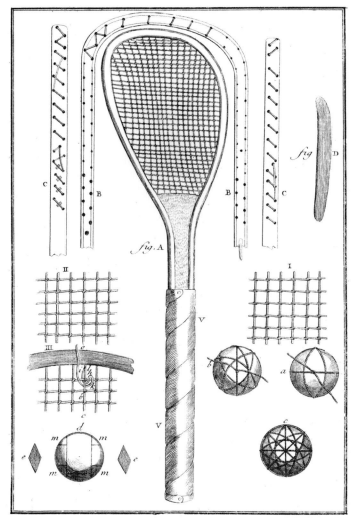

*An illustration
depicting how tennis
balls and rackets were
made in the eighteenth
century, published in
France in 1775 by
l'Académie Royale des
Sciences. (Koninklijke
Bibliothek, Den Haag)*

Chris Ronaldson, the head professional at Hampton Court Palace, makes a tennis ball.

barely bounced at all. In fact, they could be quite dangerous. In the fifteenth century the standard of ball-making in France was so bad that Louis XI decreed that all balls be stuffed with good hide and wool; the use of sand, chalk, ash or sawdust was prohibited. Later balls were made of felt or rubber round a small billet of iron and covered with leather. Today the Tuscan players of *pallaeh!* use a pellet of lead for the centre of their balls, as balls that have their weight concentrated in the centre are much better.

There have been many other ways of making balls. Leather balls filled with animal or human hair are referred to by Shakespeare and this method is still used today in the Dutch game *kaatsen*. Evidence of wooden balls bound with leather from the eighteenth century has been found in France and England, and there are also references to the 'wind ball' and the 'yarn ball' (the latter being a ball of woollen yarn wrapped round a suitable centre). In 1960 Dunlop invented a ball-making machine but the balls it produced were never quite as good as the hand-made ones.

Present-day balls are made, still by hand, by putting cork into a used felt sack, which is then bound with linen thread. This core is then wrapped in about 6 metres of half-inch cotton webbing and tied with linen thread. The symmetry of this tying determines how spherical the ball will be. Finally, strips of white or yellow woollen felt are tacked on and sewn together by hand, the whole process taking over half an hour. A perfect ball must weigh between 71 and

A racket and ball.

78 grams and have a diameter of between 62 and 65 mm.

A royal set comprises six dozen balls, so there are usually seventy-two balls on the court at any one time. Each set lasts about 150 hours, or between ten and thirty days depending on the level of court usage, before the covers of the balls are worn out. The process of re-tying balls and replacing the felt covers is a time-consuming daily routine for the professionals attached to the various clubs. In 1499 the Ironmongers' Company, which made tennis balls for the London courts, was charging one shilling a gross. In 2004 balls cost £12.00 each.

Rackets

His present, and your pains, we thank you for:
When we have match'd our rackets to these balls,
We will, in France, by God's grace, play a set
Shall strike his father's crown into the hazard.
Tell him he hath made a match with such a wrangler
That all the courts of France will be disturb'd
With chases.

William Shakespeare, *King Henry V*, Act 1, Scene 1

Tennis was originally played with the bare hand, from which comes
the French name for the game, *jeu de paume* ('game with the palm of
the hand'). Later, hands were bound to protect them and gloves

Sievemakers, from 'Het Menselyk Bedryf' ('The Book of Trades') by Jan Luyken, 1694. Sieves were used for serving the ball in some forms of the game, and tennis rackets may have developed from them. (Koninklijke Bibliotheek, Den Haag)

An 1879 prize racket from Oxford.

were worn by wealthier players. Some games today still use gloves, sometimes with a plate on the palm, as in *kaatsen*, where the plate is plastic. In other games the plate is made of steel.

The origins of the racket are not certain but it is thought that it arose through the use of a sieve for serving the ball in some forms of the game. One day somebody must have picked up the sieve and discovered that the ball could be projected a long way with it. In France the head of the racket is called *le tamis*, 'the sieve'. This could also explain why the earlier rackets were strung diagonally. The word 'racket' probably comes from the French *rachasser* or *racacher*, meaning 'to return the ball'. The earlier rackets had very short handles. Although present-day rackets have longer handles they are not held at the end but a little way down the shaft.

Early rackets were constructed from strips of wood that were made pliable by either steaming them or soaking them in copper baths. These strips were then bent round a frame that gave them their distinctive shape. A centrepiece of soft wood was inserted between the strips and strengthened with the fibre of tendons taken from an ox's foot. The first rackets were strung by wrapping the cross strings around the vertical, thus creating a rough side and a smooth side, but from the nineteenth century the strings were interwoven, giving much more tension and striking power to the rackets. Modern rackets are still made of wood and built to an asymmetric specification, so that the head of the racket resembles a hand. Over the centuries rackets were made by sievemakers and brushmakers before specialist racket makers took over the task. Now only one racket manufacturer, Grays of Cambridge, founded in 1855, still makes real tennis rackets, supplying about three thousand frames

per year to the various clubs around the world, where the professionals string the rackets.

The major development since the 1970s has been in the move from sheep-gut (not the cat-gut of legend) to a synthetic cord, which can maintain much higher tension. This has led to a considerably faster game, especially at the top levels. However, real tennis has resisted the move to graphite or metallic rackets which has had such a radical effect on its junior counterpart, lawn tennis.

The court and the rules

To the Tennis Court and there saw the King play at Tennis, and others; but to see how the King's play was extolled without any case at all was a loathsome sight, though sometimes he did play very well and deserved to be commended; but such open flattery is beastly.

Samuel Pepys, 1664

Every real tennis court in the world is unique. Although they all have a tambour, grille, galleries and penthouses (apart from the oldest court of all, at Falkland Palace in Fife, which is a *jeu quarré*), each court is slightly different in its overall size, in the angles of the penthouses and tambour, and in the size of the galleries. This means that playing on your home court has huge advantages. The court at Hampton Court Palace is a particularly large one, measuring 29 metres by 10 metres on the floor. This is bigger than the playing area of a modern lawn tennis court, which is 24 metres by 11 metres.

Imagine you have entered the court and are standing by the net post under the side penthouse, which is where the marker stands ('marker' is the term used in real tennis for the umpire). To your left is the hazard end of the court, with four galleries on your immediate

Falkland Palace court in Fife, the oldest court in Britain. This is a jeu quarré court, which means it has no conventional dedans or dedans penthouse and no tambour. The photograph is taken from the hazard end. The four rectangular holes are called 'lunes'.

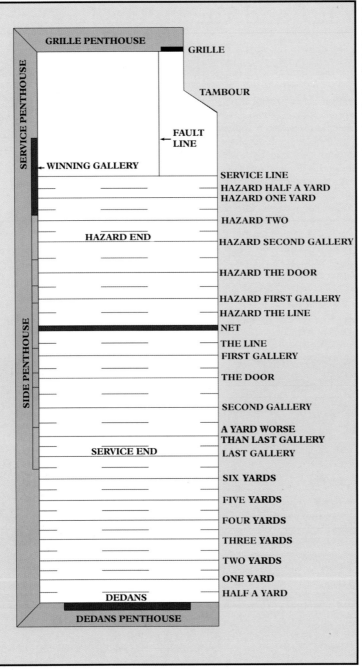

GRILLE PENTHOUSE

GRILLE

SERVICE PENTHOUSE

TAMBOUR

FAULT
LINE

WINNING GALLERY

SERVICE LINE
HAZARD HALF A YARD
HAZARD ONE YARD

HAZARD TWO

HAZARD END

HAZARD SECOND GALLERY

HAZARD THE DOOR

HAZARD FIRST GALLERY
HAZARD THE LINE

NET

SIDE PENTHOUSE

THE LINE
FIRST GALLERY

THE DOOR

SECOND GALLERY

A YARD WORSE
THAN LAST GALLERY

SERVICE END

LAST GALLERY

SIX YARDS

FIVE YARDS

FOUR YARDS

THREE YARDS

TWO YARDS

ONE YARD

DEDANS

HALF A YARD

DEDANS PENTHOUSE

Plan of a real tennis court. The long lines on the floor are chase lines; the short lines merely mark half yards. The galleries are under the side and service penthouses. A ball hit into the grille, the winning gallery or the dedans is a winning shot.

Right: *The court at Hampton Court Palace from the service end, showing the penthouse running round three sides of the court and the grille at the hazard end.*

Below: *The court at Hampton Court Palace from the hazard end, showing the galleries and also the dedans behind the server. The door on to the court is in the alcove by the net post and this is where the marker stands to mark a match.*

left, called respectively first, door, second and winning galleries. In the far opposite corner from where you are standing is the grille, and on the long wall (main wall) facing you is a buttress called the tambour. On the floor running from the galleries to the main wall are chase lines.

To your right is the service end of the court. On your immediate right are four more galleries, first, door, second and last galleries. At the far end of the court is a long large gallery called the dedans, with a sloping roof, or penthouse, above it. This penthouse runs round three sides of the court. There are chase lines covering the whole of the service end. In England these are yard lines measured from the back wall (the markings are slightly different on French courts). A line runs round the top of the whole court; any ball touching the wall on or above that line or the very high roof is out of play.

You serve only from the service side, but this can be from anywhere in the back two-thirds of the service end. The service must touch the penthouse on the hazard side and bounce in the back half of the hazard court, i.e between the back wall, the service line and the fault line. After the service all the walls and penthouses are in play, though it is normally best to keep the ball as low as possible. Hitting a ball into the winning gallery and the grille are both winning

Chris Bray, the professional at Petworth, Sussex.

strokes, and hitting the tambour creates a difficult shot for your opponent. Consequently it is tremendously advantageous to be at the service end. The receiving player only has one winning shot, which is into the dedans.

The scoring is 15, 30, 40, deuce, advantage and game; lawn tennis took its marking system straight from real tennis. However, in the ancient game it is the first person to six games who wins the set.

The chase is the hardest part of the scoring to understand. When a player fails to hit a ball, the point where the ball bounces for the second time is noted. If this second bounce lands anywhere where there are chase lines, that place is recorded. The point is then held in abeyance until game point, when the players change ends. Let us say the ball bounced for the second time on chase four and the players changed ends. The player now at the hazard, or receiving, end has to play each stroke of the next point in such a way that the ball would bounce for the second time closer to the back wall than chase four. The server for his or her part has to decide whether to leave the ball, because the second bounce is going to be more than 4 yards from the back wall (in which case he wins the point), or to hit it, because it is going to bounce closer to the back wall than the 4 yard line, thereby keeping the ball in play. Thus chase one is a very difficult chase to beat from the hazard end whereas chase second gallery is

Bernard Weatherill plays a forehand drive down the main wall at his home court, the Royal Tennis Court at Hampton Court Palace, during the Field Trophy, a knockout inter-club championship. A spectator can be seen watching in the dedans.

quite an easy one. Players only change ends at game point when a chase has been set, or immediately when two chases have been set. If no chases are set in a game the players do not change ends and the original server continues to serve.

Spectators usually sit in the dedans: behind the netting there are commonly a couple of rows of seats where spectators can sit in safety. Sometimes for matches (and depending on the court) there is also seating down the side galleries. All the galleries are netted. Glazed or partly glazed walls, such as the ones at Cambridge University, Prested Hall in Essex, Washington DC, and Newport, Rhode Island, are ideal for those watching.

Real tennis has been likened to playing chess on a tennis court and certainly there is huge skill in placing the ball, setting chases and using the angles of the wall. It takes a long time to learn the intricacies of the game, and the weight of the racket makes it a difficult game for youngsters to master. Many a wily older player can beat a younger inexperienced competitor and it is no coincidence that world champions are usually in their thirties or early forties.

Tennis is an exhilarating game to watch too, with long rallies and balls played close to the floor with a lot of cut and spin. Balls can reach speeds of 225 km per hour (140 miles per hour), but a skilful player can use that speed and the angles of the court to his or her advantage. In addition there are forty different serves from which to choose: the giraffe, the railroad, the boomerang, the bobble, the drag and the caterpillar are

Guy Smith-Bingham, a member of Queen's Club, plays a backhand slice during the Field Trophy. Chase lines are clearly visible on the floor.

David Watson and Fred Satow,
members of the Royal Tennis Court,
playing doubles in the Field Trophy
at Moreton Morrell. Fred Satow is
standing in front of the grille at the
hazard end. The painted crowns
denote the lines on the hazard end.
The far one is the fault line; the near
one is used only in doubles.

some of the more colourful names for these.

Doubles, which used to be known as the four-handed game, is very popular at some courts, particularly those in the USA. The tactics for doubles play are rather different. In singles the best tactic is to hit low into the corner. In doubles there is somebody standing in each corner, so doubles play involves more shots down the middle of the court, more volleying, and more attempts at hitting the winning targets: it is, at top levels, a very fast and exciting game to play and to watch.

European ball games

Here you may commonly see artisans, such as hatters, playing tennis for a crown,
which is not often seen elsewhere, particularly on a working day.

Etienne Pasquier, on a visit to England, 1558

Italy

In the 1980s Roger Morgan came across a ball game in Tuscany that changed his thinking on the origins of real tennis. The game is called *pallaeh!* or *pallaventuno* and is played in a few hilltop Tuscan villages between Siena and Grosseto. (*Palla* means ball, and *eh!* is the call made by the server to warn the receivers that the ball is on the way; *ventuno*, or twenty-one, refers to the scoring system, which is 7, 14 and 21). There are many differences between tennis and *pallaeh!*. For instance, the Tuscans use their hand (bare or with a glove) and the ball is much smaller. However, Roger Morgan also saw similarities, the most striking being the use of chases, marking where the ball finished bouncing, and the scoring system. *Pallaeh!* also makes use of any walls, balconies or staircases (or even hapless onlookers) in the vicinity. The balls are made by the players and consist of a pellet of lead wrapped in rubber, then bound with wool yarn and covered with leather. The court markings are painted

A player serves in
pallaeh! at
Scalvaia. The
scoreboard can be
seen behind him.

A player holding a hand-made pallaeh! ball.

permanently on the road, and the chases are marked on the ground with chalk. Thus there are huge differences between each 'court' and consequently a great advantage in playing at home. The receiving players often cannot see the serve and must stand searching the sky for the ball. Play stops briefly when a car needs to pass through.

Other games found in Italy include *pallone*, played in the Rimini area with a hard rubber ball and a *bracciale*, a wooden cylinder used to strike the ball and protect the forearm. *Pallone elastico*, also from Italy, is played in the Piedmont region with a bandaged fist. It uses chases and a tennis system of scoring.

Below: *Pallaeh! The photograph was taken from near where the server stands. The ball can just be seen flying towards the roof of the church. The players have to follow the trajectory of the ball as far as possible. If it disappears out of sight they have to guess where and when it will come down.*

The trinquet court at Guethary near Biarritz, France.

France

In the Basque region *pelote basque* is *the* sport. Every village has a *fronton*, an open-air playing area with a solid wall at the front (always painted pink) and seats for spectators along the sides. Some are quite short, but others can be 100 metres long. Most towns will have a *trinquet*, an indoor court, 9.3 metres wide and nearly 30 metres long. Sometimes one of the long walls is made of glass and behind this people can sit at tables or at a bar to eat and drink while watching. The *trinquet* court has a gallery running most of the length of one long wall, and a small buttress in one corner of the front wall. In a few towns there are large indoor courts called *murs à gauche*, 9.5 metres wide and 36 metres long.

There are about twenty-two forms of *pelote basque* played on these three courts. The *trinquet* is used for several very distinct games, using different rackets or gloves and different balls. The main ones are *main nue*, *paleta gomme*, *xare* and *paleta cuir*, but others such as *paleta pelote de gomme* and *pasaka* can be found. *Rebot*, which uses the basketweave scoop called the *chistera*, *pala corta* and *pala larga* are three of the games played on the *frontons* and *murs à gauche*.

Balle-pelote and *balle au gant* are played in northern France and Belgium, using the tennis scoring system and chases. The Belgian *balle-pelote* is played with a softer ball and only a thin glove on a court 60–70 metres long, whereas *balle au gant* uses a harder ball and a thicker glove on a larger court 80–100 metres long.

The *jeu de longue paume* is played in northern France: like *rebot* it is played on a large open area, but rackets are used.

Rebot being played on a fronton in the Basque region of France. The service is made by bouncing the ball on the butoir, which throws the ball forward.

Spain

The same games are played in the Basque region of Spain as in the French Basque region.

Pilota valenciana and *raspall* are played in the villages in Valencia. In *pilota* the ball is made of leather triangles stuffed with wool flock and in both sports players spend a lot of time bandaging their hands before a game for protection. *Galotxa* also used to be played in the Valencian streets, but courts, or *galotxetes*, have been built to avoid the inconvenience of playing in the street.

Llargues is the simplest and probably the oldest of all *jeux de*

Rackets or gloves and balls used in the different games played on a trinquet court. (Left to right) Chistera, paleta pelote de cuir, paleta pelote de gomme, and xare.

Jeu de longue paume, 1655.

Balle au gant at Brussels in Belgium from 'Le Globe Illustré'. Note the sieve, which is no longer used for serving.

A glove and ball used in kaatsen, from the Kaatsen Museum at Franeker in Holland.

paume. It is played in the streets in the area around Alicante and resembles the Tuscan game *pallaeh!*.

Holland

Kaatsen is played in Friesland in northern Holland and each year the finals in August attract a huge crowd of spectators. There are three players in a team and they use a small hard ball stuffed with hair, which they strike using a gloved hand. After the first bounce the players are also allowed to kick the ball. A *kaats* is a chase.

This is by no means a complete list of the games that are played around Europe but simply an overview to show the variety that exists. Similar ball games have also crossed the Atlantic and have been seen in Colombia, Ecuador, Mexico and the Canaries. It is interesting to note that many (though not all) of these sports thrive in areas where minority languages and culture exist within a larger state, for instance in the Basque region of France, Catalonia in Spain and Friesland in Holland.

Victims, villains and heroes

We are merely the stars' tennis balls, struck and bandied which way please them.
John Webster, *The Duchess of Malfi*, Act 5, Scene 4

Let us deal first with the victims. One of the most startling was the tennis opponent of the baroque painter Michelangelo Caravaggio in 1606. Caravaggio lost the game, stabbed his opponent and was forced into exile. He never returned to Rome.

Several kings and princes have died because of a tennis game. Charles VIII of France hit his head on a door lintel of the tennis court at Amboise in 1498 and died. In the thirteenth and fourteenth centuries Henry I of Castile and Louis X and Philip IV of France are all reputed to have come off court after a game of tennis, drunk a beaker of cold water, caught pneumonia and died soon after. Henry, Prince of Wales, James I's heir, also caught a chill while playing tennis in October 1612 and died a month later.

James I of Scotland was murdered in 1437 while he was staying at the Blackfriars monastery at Perth. He attempted to escape through the sewer but that route had been blocked three days earlier on his own orders because it was connected to the tennis court and balls kept disappearing down 'that fowle hole'. He had to turn back and was killed.

The heir of the Stanley family in Elford, Staffordshire, died sometime between 1470 and 1480 of a blow to the temple by a tennis ball. His tomb can be seen in the parish church, showing him holding a tennis ball in one hand and pointing to his temple with the other. The inscription reads *'Ubi dolor, ibi digitus'* ('My finger points to where the pain is').

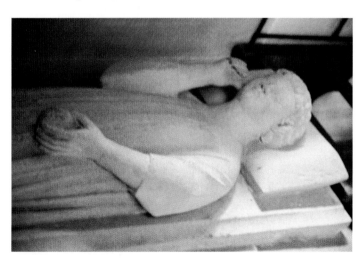

The tomb of the Stanley boy in Elford church, Staffordshire.

The painting of Henry VIII on the grille at the club at Hampton Court Palace by Lesley Ronaldson and other artists of the Centre d'Arte Verrocchio.

While Anne Boleyn was watching, and betting on, a game of tennis at Whitehall she was arrested and taken to the Tower, to be beheaded a few weeks later, in 1536. Thirty years later David Rizzio, the Italian secretary of Mary, Queen of Scots, was murdered by Lord Darnley hours after he had played tennis with Darnley.

On a happier note there is a story about François I, king of France in the first half of the sixteenth century: 'a certain Monk while playing with the King against two lords, made a brilliant stroke which decided the set in the King's favour'. The King then exclaimed, 'Ah, that is the stroke of a Monk.' 'Sire,' replied the monk, 'whenever it may please you, it shall be the stroke of an Abbot.' Fortunately an abbey happened to be vacant and the monk was duly made its abbot.

A towering figure in tennis, in more ways than one, was Henry VIII. He was very athletic as a young man and loved all sports, especially tennis. He must have played on Cardinal Wolsey's 'open play' while Hampton Court Palace still belonged to Wolsey; when Henry took over the property in 1528 he had a 'closed play' built about 100 metres further south. Charles I built the present court at Hampton Court Palace on the site of Wolsey's original court as one of his first acts upon succeeding to the throne in 1625.

Today the royal connection with the game is continued by Prince Edward, Earl of Wessex, who is an enthusiastic player. He met his

Above: *'Le Serment du jeu de paume à Versailles le 20 juin 1789'* by *Jacques-Louis David. The painting depicts a significant event in the French Revolution, the swearing of an oath at the Versailles tennis court. (Musée des Châteaux de Versailles et Trianon)*

future wife, Sophie, in 1993 at Queen's Club, London, during a press conference for his twelve-hour real tennis marathon at Holyport, which raised £20,000 for charity.

In France *le jeu de paume* has been made famous by the oath that was sworn on the Versailles tennis court by members of the self-styled National Assembly on 20th June 1789, during the early days of the French Revolution. They met in the Salle du Jeu de Paume in defiance of the King, who had excluded them from a building normally used for meetings.

An outstanding player of the eighteenth century was Raymond Masson, who also had the unusual distinction, for those days, of a wife who played good tennis herself.

There have been some outstanding men's champions among the twenty-four that the game has produced (the first was Clergé in 1740). Edmond J. Barre of France was

Edmond Barre, the world champion from 1829 to 1862.

Tom Pettitt, the first American world champion, from 1885 to 1890. He invented the railroad serve, a fast overarm service that runs the length of the penthouse with a reverse twist.

The British player Peter Latham, the world champion of both rackets (1887–1902) and tennis (1895–1905, 1907–8).

An oil painting by Shelly Bancroft of the Basque player Pierre Etchebaster, the world champion between 1928 and 1954, when he retired undefeated.

champion from 1829 to 1862, at thirty-three years the longest reign on record. It is said that he used to walk twenty miles to play an exhibition match, win and then walk twenty miles back again. His terms for coming to England to play exhibitions were his fees, his expenses and 'two wenches a day'.

The first great American champion was Tom Pettitt, the inventor of the railroad serve, who was world champion from 1885 to 1890, when he resigned after defeating Charles Saunders. He challenged for the title again in 1898 but was defeated by the great British player Peter Latham, who was world champion of both rackets (1887–1902) and tennis (1895–1905 and again 1907–8).

The eccentric Basque player Pierre Etchebaster won the title in 1928 at the

Chris Ronaldson, the world champion from 1981 to 1987.

Lachie Deuchar, who was considered the best player in the world in 1990 and 1991.

ripe old age of thirty-four but, amazingly, retained it until he was almost sixty, when he retired undefeated in 1954. He continued to play and coach into his eighties. The British player Jim Dear was champion from 1955 to 1957. He is particularly remembered for having also held the world squash and rackets titles. Chris Ronaldson, world champion from 1981 to 1987, was the first player to win the Grand Slam in one year (British, French, Australian and US Open tournaments).

In 1990 and 1991 Lachie Deuchar was considered the best player in the world, having incurred no singles losses in those two years.

Since then the outstanding men's champion has been the Australian Rob Fahey, who has taken advantage of slight changes in equipment (stronger rackets and synthetic strings) to develop a game that suits his extraordinary power and athleticism. He won the title in 1994.

Ladies' tennis

But canstow playen raket, to and fro.

Geoffrey Chaucer, *Troilus and Criseyde*, Book 4

In 1981 Lesley Ronaldson, British ladies' champion from 1979 to 1981 and in 1986, founded the Ladies' Real Tennis Association and led it for its first ten years. The first world championship, played not as a challenge but as a tournament, was won by the Australian Judy Clarke in 1985. Since 1989 the championship has been dominated by Penny Lumley. Between 1989 and 2004 she won six of the eight world championships and twelve British Open championships. She is equally impressive as a doubles player, in the same period winning six world doubles titles and nine British Open doubles titles. In 1996–7 she held all the major titles, winning the British, French, American and Australian Open tournaments as well as the world singles and doubles titles.

Lesley Ronaldson, a former British ladies' champion and founder of the Ladies' Real Tennis Association.

Penny Lumley MBE, who has dominated the game since 1989.

Real tennis today

Let other people play at other things;
The King of Games is still the Game of Kings.

J. K. Stephen, 'Parker's Piece', 1891

Great Britain

There are twenty-nine courts in Britain, although three of these are hardly ever used. Queen's Club in London, Cambridge University and Prested Hall in Essex have two courts each. More importantly, new courts have been built and old courts reopened, and those courts which are in play have seen their usage expand from an hour or two a day to full capacity. At Hampton Court, for example, which is open 364 days of the year, the first court is often booked at seven in the morning and it is quite common for people to be playing until eleven o'clock at night.

The sport is increasing in popularity among young players. Three schools already have real tennis courts and several other schools, both state and private, have made, are making or are considering making similar applications to build courts.

The court at Hampton Court Palace from the east front.

The court at Bordeaux, France. The court markings are slightly different in France, representing the ancient French foot (about 14 inches or 36 cm).

France

There are only three courts in use in France today. The famous seventeenth-century court of Fontainebleau was out of commission for many decades in the twentieth century and was restored only in 1990. The court in Paris was built in the late nineteenth century; it has, in fact, two courts but one of these has been converted into four squash courts. There are still 106 courts recognisable in Paris, among them the Jeu de Paume (near the Louvre), which used to house the country's Impressionist art collection. The current court in Bordeaux is the twentieth known to have been built in the city and was completed in 1978.

Australia

Australia has six courts. Although there are records of a court being built in Ballarat in the 1860s, the oldest surviving court is the Hobart court in Tasmania, dating back to 1875. The original Melbourne court was built in 1882 in the centre of the city but in

Hobart court, Tasmania, using a wide-angle lens.

Prince's Court, Washington, showing the spectacular glass wall.

1974 this valuable property was sold and two new courts built in the suburb of Richmond. The present Ballarat court was built in 1984, that in Sydney in 1997 and Romsey's in 1999.

United States of America

There are ten courts in the USA, all on the eastern seaboard and all built at the end of the nineteenth century or later. From north to south these are Boston, Massachusetts; Newport, Rhode Island; Tuxedo Park, New York; New York City (two courts); Greentree, Long Island; Lakewood, New Jersey; Philadelphia; Washington; and Aiken, South Carolina.

Ireland and Holland

In 2004 both Holland and Ireland have real tennis associations but no court. The Irish club is trying to reopen the court built by Sir Edward Guinness in 1885 where the 1890 World Championship match took place between Tom Pettitt and Charles Saunders. Holland is still looking for a suitable venue.

A game which looked as if it was foundering in 1970 is once more going from strength to strength. New courts are being built or reinstated, and existing courts are busy. International matches are played regularly and ladies' tennis is becoming more and more popular. Many courts are also active in encouraging their younger members, so that a new generation of players is coming up through the ranks. Competitions, intra-club and inter-club, are run by all clubs at all levels. The future looks bright.

Further reading

Several books have been published by Ronaldson Publications, 13A Linkside Avenue, Oxford OX2 8HY (website: www.ronaldsonpublications.com):

Barcellon, Pierre. *Rules and Principles of Tennis.* 1987.
Best, David. *The Royal Tennis Court.* 2002.
Covey, Neil (editor). *Fred Covey, World Champion of Tennis.* 1994.
Howell, Jonathan. *More Than a Yard Worse.* 1995.
Morgan, Roger. *Tennis: The Development of the European Ball Game.* 1994.
Morgan, Roger. *Tudor Tennis: A Miscellany.* 2001.
Ronaldson, Chris. *Tennis: A Cut Above the Rest* (book and video). 1998.
Shneerson, John. *Two Centuries of Real Tennis.* 1997.
Wade, Charles. *The History of the Leamington Tennis Court Club.* 1996.

Books published by other publishers:
Aberdare, Lord. *The J. T. Faber Book of Tennis and Rackets.* Quiller Press, 2001.
Bonhomme, Guy. *De la Paume au Tennis.* 1991.
Butler, L. St. J., and Wordie, P. J. (editors). *The Royal Game.* Falkland Palace Real Tennis Club, 1989.
Danzig, Allison. *The Winning Gallery.* 1985.
Garnett, Michael. *A History of Royal Tennis in Australia.* Historical Publications, 1985.
Gillmeister, Heiner. *Tennis: A Cultural History.* Cassell Academic/Leicester University Press, 1997.
Potter, Jeremy. *Tennis and Oxford.* Oxford Unicorn Press, 1994.

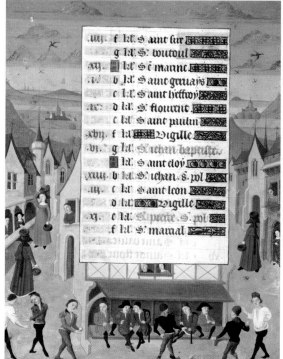

An illustration from the Book of Hours of the Duchess of Burgundy (month of June), northern French, c.1450, showing a game of tennis, with spectators under the sloping roof behind. (Bibliothèque de Musée Condé, Château de Chantilly)

Courts in use and governing bodies

United Kingdom
Governing body: *The Tennis and Rackets Association*, c/o the Queen's Club, Palliser Road, West Kensington, London W14 9EQ. Telephone: 020 7386 3447/8. Website: www.queensclub.co.uk

Bristol and Bath Tennis Club, Beggar Bush Playing Fields, Abbots Leigh Road, Bristol BS8 3QD. Telephone: 0117 973 3444. Website: www.bbtennis.org.uk
The Burroughs Club, Middlesex University, Hendon, London NW4 4JF. Telephone: 020 8411 6768. Website: www.mdx.ac.uk/realtennis
Cambridge University Tennis Court, The Tennis Court, Grange Road, Cambridge CB3 9DJ. Telephone: 01223 357106. Website: www.curtc.net
Canford School, Wimborne Minster, Dorset BH21 3AD. Telephone: 01202 881232. Website: www.canford.com
Falkland Palace Royal Tennis Court, Falkland, Cupar, Fife KY15 7BU. Telephone: 01337 857397. Website: http://forth.stir.ac.uk/~pmbc1/flklnd.htm
The Harbour Club, Watermeadow Lane, London SW6 2RR. Telephone: 020 7751 9411. Website: www.harbourclub.co.uk
Hardwick House, Whitchurch, near Reading, Berkshire RG8 7RB. Telephone: 01491 681306.
Hatfield House Tennis Club, c/o Fore Street Lodge, Hatfield House, Old Hatfield, Hertfordshire AL9 5NF. Telephone: 01707 273391. Website: www.hhtc.net
Holyport Real Tennis Club, Holyport Street, Holyport, near Maidenhead, Berkshire SL6 2JR. Telephone: 01628 673964.
The Hyde Tennis Club, Walditch, Bridport, Dorset DT6 4LB. Telephone: 01308 420777.
The Leamington Tennis Court Club, 50 Bedford Street, Leamington Spa, Warwickshire CV32 5DT. Telephone: 01926 424977. Website: www.leamington-tennis-squash.co.uk
The Manchester Tennis and Racquet Club, 33 Blackfriars Road, Salford, Manchester M3 7AQ. Telephone: 0161 834 0616.
MCC, The Tennis Court, Lord's Ground, St John's Wood, London NW8 8QN. Telephone: 020 7616 8685. Website: www.lords.org
Moreton Morrell Tennis Court Club, Moreton Morrell, Warwickshire CV35 9AL. Telephone: 01926 651229.
Newcastle upon Tyne Real Tennis Club, Matthew Bank, Jesmond, Newcastle upon Tyne NE2 3RE. Telephone: 0191 281 6854.
The Newmarket and Suffolk Real Tennis Club, Fitzroy Street, Newmarket CB8 0JW. Telephone: 01638 666612.
The Oratory Tennis Club, The Sports Centre, The Oratory School, Woodcote, near Reading, Berkshire RG8 0PJ. Telephone: 01491 681303. Website: www.oratorytennisclub.net
Oxford University Tennis Court, c/o Merton College, Merton Street, Oxford OX1 4JD. Telephone: 01865 244212. Website: www.outc.org.uk
Petworth House Tennis Court, Estate Yard, Petworth House, Petworth, Sussex GU28 0DU. Telephone: 01798 343527.
The Prested Hall Racket Club, Prested Hall, Feering, near Kelvedon, Essex CO5 9EE. Telephone: 01376 570220. Website: www.prested.com
The Queen's Club, Palliser Road, West Kensington, London W14 9EQ. Telephone: 020 7385 3421. Website: www.queensclub.co.uk
The Royal Tennis Court, Hampton Court Palace, East Molesey, Surrey KT8 9AU. Telephone: 020 8977 3015. Website: www.realtennis.gbrit.com
Seacourt Tennis Club, Victoria Avenue, Hayling Island, Hampshire PO11 9AJ. Telephone: 023 9246 6122. Website: www.seacourt.com

France

Governing body: *Comité Français du Jeu de Courte Paume*, 19 rue de Varennes, 75007 Paris. Telephone: +33 1 45 49 16 82.

Cercle du Jeu de Paume de Fontainebleau, Palais Nationale, 77300 Fontainebleau. Telephone: +33 1 64 22 47 67.
Jeu de Paume et Squash de Bordeaux, 369 Avenue de Verdun, 33700 Mérignac. Telephone: +33 556 97 51 12.
Société Sportive du Jeu de Paume et de Racquets, 74 Ter Rue Lauriston, 75016 Paris. Telephone: +33 1 47 27 46 86. Website: www.paume-squash-paris.com

Australia

Governing body: *Australian Real Tennis Association*, c/o Royal Melbourne Tennis Club, 18 Sherwood Street, Richmond, Victoria 3121. Telephone: +61 3 9429 9788.

The Ballarat Tennis Club, Larter Street, Ballarat, Victoria 3350. Telephone: +61 3 5333 5755. Website: www.ballarattennisclub.com
Cope-Williams Real Tennis Club, Glenfern Road, Romsey, Victoria 3434. Telephone: +61 3 54 296222. Website: www.cope-williams.com.au
The Hobart Tennis Club, 45 Davey Street, Hobart, Tasmania 7000. Telephone: +61 3 6231 1781. Website: www.hobarttennis.com.au
The Royal Melbourne Tennis Club, 18 Sherwood Street, Richmond, Victoria 3121. Telephone: +61 3 9429 9788.
The Sydney Real Tennis Club, Macquarie University Sports Union, Macquarie University, Sydney, New South Wales 2109. Telephone: +61 2 9850 9495. Website: www.sydneyrealtennis.com.au

USA

Governing body: *The United States Court Tennis Association*, 21 Hamilton Avenue, Jamestown, Rhode Island 02835. Telephone/fax: +1 401 423 3841.

The Aiken Tennis Club, 146 Newberry Street SW, Aiken, South Carolina 29802. Telephone: +1 803 648 2152.
The Georgian Court, Georgian Court College, Lakewood, New Jersey 08701. Telephone: +1 215 854 6014. Website: www.georgian.edu
The Greentree Court, Long Island (private court).
The International Tennis Club of Washington (Prince's Court), 1800 Old Meadow Road, Mclean, Virginia 22102. Telephone: +1 703 556 6550. Website: www.princescourt.com
The National Tennis Club, 194 Bellevue Avenue, Newport, Rhode Island 02840. Telephone: +1 401 849 6672. Website: www.nationaltennisclub.org
The Racquet and Tennis Club, 370 Park Avenue, New York 10022. Telephone: +1 212 753 9700.
The Racquet Club of Philadelphia, 215 South 16th Street, Philadelphia, Pennsylvania 19102. Telephone: +1 215 735 1525. Website: www.rcop.com
The Tennis and Racquet Club, 939 Boylston Street, Boston, Massachusetts 02115. Telephone: +1 617 536 4630. Website: www.tandr.org
The Tuxedo Club, Tuxedo Park, New York 10987. Telephone: +1 845 351 4791.

The International Real Tennis Professionals Association is at 43 Montholme Road, London SW11 6HX. Telephone: 020 8333 4267. It has a useful website: www.irtpa.com

Index